from
Laura
Christmas
2003

Sister

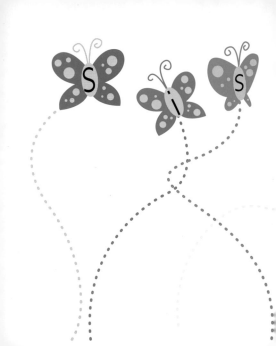

t e r

Margaret Lannamann

Illustrated by Lisa Parett

Ariel Books

**Andrews McMeel Publishing**

Kansas City

Illustrations copyright © 2003 by Lisa Parett

ISBN: 0-7407-3373-7
Library of Congress Control Number: 2002111888

*For Cynthia*

# intro

Our sisters: Who else knows about all of our embarrassing moments and disastrous relationships and loves us anyway? Who else comforts us when we're down and persuades us that our new "fashionable" haircut isn't so bad after all? And who else joins us in true celebration when something wonderful happens?

Sister

# duction

Whether they're across the room or across the ocean, our sisters serve as our comfort, our support, our strongest fans—and sometimes our toughest critics. We dedicate this little book to them, with thanks and love, for the friendship and the laughter they bring into our lives.

We are sisters. We will always be sisters. Our differences may never go away, but neither, for me, will our song.

—Nancy Kelton

Sister

We are linked by blood, and blood is memory without language.

—Joyce Carol Oates

# Your relationship with your

S i s t e r

t e r

is a

c o n v e r s a t i o n .

11

## Success Simply Being Sisters

The Satellite Sisters (Julie, Liz, Sheila, Monica, and Lian Dolan) have a popular **talk show** on National Public Radio. While growing up, the sisters honed their act "doing the endless dishes for a family of ten. . . . Night after night, we **washed**, talked,

*Sister*

laughed. . . . . We had no entertainment career aspirations, just hope that someday our mother would fix the dishwasher." But those conversations, they insist, were the basis for the lively, humorous, and entertaining program they host today.

13

A Sister Is

When you're a teenager, you think your sister is a pest. She takes your clothes, bothers you when you're on the phone, and won't *ever* leave you alone. But as you get older, she becomes your best friend, and later, you realize that a lot of the things you look for in a new friend you already have in a sister.

—*Alex, Atlanta, Georgia*

"The girls," we were referred to by our family as if tied by the same umbilical cord. If one moved, the other was bound to follow.

—Patricia Foster

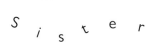

Sister

Growing up, we argued about everything. Now we have conversations instead.

—Patricia Bundchen

It is to be treasured when sisters are close or best friends, and what a loss for both of them when they aren't.

—Linda Bucklin and Mary Keil

Sister

The sound of her voice res-
onates with the sounds of our lives,
of our children, our hopes,
our history.

—*Judy Collins*

19

W<sub>e</sub> *never* get

S i s t e r

tired of each other.

—*Venus Williams,*
*about her sister Serena*

They were so **bound** together
that as small children, when they slept
in the same crib, they awak-
ened every morning each sucking
the other's thumb.

—Kaye Gibbons

Sister

When we were young, we believed that if we slept with our heads touching, we would dream the same dream.

—Lisa Kalis

As my sister has so often reminded me, I am not her and she is not me. We see the world differently . . .

—Joan Wickersham

Sister

Sisters are like different instruments in a band, or different voices in a chorus: Because you are not exactly alike, you harmonize in beautiful ways.

Sisters: friends, cheer-
leaders, confidantes.

Value: immeasurable.

Importance: infinite.

Life expectancy: forever.

I'm so *happy*
that I have my

# s i s t

*S i s t e r*

ers.

I can see us *growing old* together.

—Allison Oki

In the 1860s, the seven Sutherland sisters had a singing act in the **Barnum and Bailey Circus.** Although their act was a big success, it wasn't because of their music—people flocked to see them because of their amazing hair.

Sister

One of the sisters had hair that was seven feet long; collectively, the sisters' hair measured thirty-seven feet.

**W**hen we *share*

s e c

S i s t e r

r e t ,

we share *more* than words.

—*Véronique Vienne*

Even when it's been a long time since you last talked, you pick up the conversation right where you left off as if it had been just yesterday.

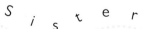

Sister

It was a happy occasion and we indulged ourselves accordingly, having exotic forms of massage, hiking in the woods, and eating our favorite candy. In real life, we were all middle-aged women; here we were just, well, sisters.

—Tracy Young

Remind yourself why you
**appreciate** them, foibles
and all.

—Roni O. Cohen

Sister

My memories give me great pleasure, enormous nourishment, whatever strength I have.

—*Lee Radziwill*

A Sister Is . . .

Sisters are built-ins. Best friends. Advice givers. Invested listeners. Extra hands for the day-to-day. Extra hearts for the crises. They don't go away. They can't. They're sisters.

—Anne, Portland, Oregon

39

They kind of give each other
**permission** to misbehave.

—*Laura Bush,*
*on her twin daughters*

S i s t e r

Mama asserted "feminist" values. She repudiated competition, encouraged us to respect one another's individuality and autonomy. We were admonished to stay out of one another's private stuff—friends, including boyfriends, were among those things that could not be shared.

—bell hooks

# Celebrity Sisters

Ashley and Wynona Judd

The Corrs: Andrea, Caroline,
and Sharon

Patricia and Roseanna Arquette

Barbara, Louise, and Irlene
Mandrell

It is amazing how two sisters can be brought up in the same family, but live very different lives.

—Joy Harjo

Sister

I realize how sweet and slippery is this word "sister"——big enough to stretch beyond biology and across time; flexible enough to define soul mates and virtual strangers . . .

—Letty Cottin Pogrebin

45

Your *sister*
is the one who will rush in
without hesitation to take care
of your kids if you need her to.

A Sister Is

Everything comes in a full circle, sisters too. You can be best friends when you're little. But then the pest stage hits. My mom used to have to separate my sister and me when we cleaned up the room we shared. It wasn't until we went off to college that I realized that my sister was actually a really great person. Once you're older, it seems you get to be best friends again.

49

—Renee, Riverside, Connecticut

Disagreements have been part of our relationship—along with forgiveness—as we are totally different personalities and love always remains.

—*Claudette Renner*

Sister

Both within the family and without,
our sisters hold up our mirrors,
our images of who we are and of who
we can dare to become.

—Elizabeth Fishel

51

Ann Landers (born Esther Friedman) and her twin sister Abby (born Pauline Friedman) of "Dear Abby" not only shared the same birthday, they also attended the same college and had a double

Sister

wedding! It is small wonder
that when one began writing advice
columns in newspapers, the other
followed suit.

But there have
always been those
Sister
Moments,
when a world ruled
by maleness was

Sister

suddenly challenged

by women who

grew up

together and then

took on that world

together.

—Patrick Giles

**S**upporting
intuitive
**S**mart

Sister

t<sub>easing</sub> e<sub>ntertaining</sub> r<sub>efreshing</sub>

teasing entertaining refreshing

A Sister Is . . .

My sisters are like gently padded bookends. Both so solidly there. The older is a mentor who believes in me more than I do myself. The younger is both adviser and floundering student-of-life. I sit cushioned between the two, safe, sound, and empowered.

—Ellin, Stamford, Connecticut

I love her in a way no one else can.
I kind of raised her and I'd do any-
thing for her.

—Wynonna Judd,
on her sister Ashley Judd

Sister

They're 100 percent responsible for where I am today—my dad, my mom, and my sister too.

—Derek Jeter

Some of the best times you have with your sister are those times when you spend time together doing absolutely nothing.

Sister

I was born on my older sister Jennifer's birthday. I don't think I was the present she was expecting that day she turned four.

—Melissa Etheridge

# Sister

*Sister*

# h o d

is like electricity. It's

an invisible but
*powerful*

connection.

—Karen Brown

A Sister Is

My sister is my lifeline. When something wonderful happens, I call her. When catastrophe strikes, I call her. As the phone is ringing, I *will* her to be there. She always is.

*Maggie, Chatham, Virginia*

67

I thoroughly and completely idol-ized my big sister. I craved her time and attention more than anyone else's. She was kind, entertaining, and thoughtful.

—Tina Sinatra,
on her sister Nancy

S i s t e r

My joy is not just in my life alone, but it's in sharing it with [my sisters].

—Allison Oki

69

Conversations with your *sister* can be the best kind of t h e r a p y

*Sister*

a p .

Never praise a sister to a sister, in the hopes of your compliments reaching the proper ears.

—Rudyard Kipling

Sister

A sister's life interrogates yours, saying, Why do you live this way? Are you doing what's right?

—Bonnie Friedman

If you don't **understand** how a woman could both **love** her sister dearly and want to **wring her neck** at the same time, then you were probably an only child.

—Linda Sunshine

Sister

Being with her is as easy as being with myself—only louder and more fun.

—Alison Kalis

We were another eternal triangle, as strong and profound a balancing act as the triangle of mother, father, and child.

—Brenda Peterson

Sister

We were like ill-assorted animals tied to a common tethering post.

—Jessica Mitford

Two's company, especially between sisters.

—Karen Brown

Sister

My sister is the confidante I could always tell every-thing to, often the plumb line of my emotions.

—Judy Collins

Book design and composition
by Diane Hobbing of
Snap-Haus Graphics
in Dumont, N J